ISRAEL
past & present

Contents:

THE HISTORY OF THE LAND OF ISRAEL

The most ancient traces of human existence in the Land of Israel, which were found in Ubeidiya near the Jordan river, are attributed to a period some 800,000 years ago (albeit taking into consideration the difficulty of precisely determining such ancient dates). Some of the findings from later periods showed resemblance to European civilizations, and some, which were affected by the extreme climatic fluctuations, are unique to the Land of Israel.

Findings from the Natufian civilization, (some 8,000 years B.C.), reveal for the first time a society that utilized food grown from plants instead of groups of food gatherers and hunters. The Ghassulian civilization, which apparently arrived from the north in the fourth millennium B.C., was typical of the Chalcolithic period - a transition period from the sole use of stone tools to metal, mainly copper and, later, bronze, implements. This civilization existed for several hundreds of years, at the beginning of which people lived in some sites in underground rooms connected by tunnels and at a later date they moved to structures on the ground. The sites that were studied revealed tools, seeds, jewelry and ritual objects. The dead were buried in the ground until only the bones remained, and then they were placed in decorated ossuaries in the shape of houses, goats etc.

At the beginning of the third millennium B.C., writing was invented and became widespread in Egypt and Mesopotamia. Another thousand years were to pass until it reached the other peoples of the area. During this period Egypt was the only political entity in the area with a central government, and it was apparently then that the foundations of the Egyptian empire were laid. The location of the Land of Israel in the center of the Eastern Mediterranean coast turned it into a central crossroads on land and sea, and an arena of conflicts between the great powers that arose and fell to the north and east, and Egypt - the dominant power in the area for thousands of years. The history of the Land of Israel is interwoven with that of Egypt, and the first written records of the Land originated in the power to the south. From these records we learn that the Egyptians periodically embarked on military campaigns to the Land of Israel in order to maintain its commercial routes and ensure tax payment and peace. During this period, fortifications first appeared in the cities, whose construction exhibits pre-

Flint arrowheads of the Neolithic period, 8th millennium B.C.

liminary planning.

The strengthening of the kingdoms to the east and north of the Land of Israel brought about military campaigns. Following these campaigns the settlement of the Land ceased. At the beginning of the second millennium B.C. the Mesopotamian Empire was consolidated under the rule of Hammurabi (1792-1750 B.C.), and included Anatolia, Syria and the Land of Israel. During this period, commerce routes were laid down, Akkadian became the language of the area and fortified cities were built with huge walls, at the highest point of which the fortress of the ruler was constructed.

From the middle of the 18th century B.C. non-Semitic peoples arrived in the area: the Hittites from the north, the Hurrians from the east, as well as Indo-Iranian tribes. This mixture of tribes who passed through the area caused far-reaching changes in all areas of life: cities were destroyed and rebuilt, building of stone walls began, and a feudal-like regime, lasting many generations, was enforced on the divided and submissive population.

Pictorial inscriptions found in Sinai, as well as examples of later writing, teach us about the changes that took place in the

Stone funerary masks of the Neolithic B period, 7th millennium B.C.

script, which became more and more linear. Finally, in the 11th century B.C. the linear script, written from right to left, became prevalent - the forefather of the Pheonician-Hebrew alphabet.

The Canaanite Period and the Israelite Settlement

The Hebrew Bible, one of the greatest books ever composed, written over the course of a thousand years, testifies to the rich inner life of the people of Israel since their beginnings. It is also a first rate historic-geographic record, the sole document from the ancient world which describes the historic courses of events, the people, the events and the places sequentially and in context of the period. This is unlike many documents which are mythical and deal with gods and deities. It is commonly held that the wrting of the Bible (in contrast to the oral traditions) was begun in the period of King David, and therefore the preceding periods are presented as they were preserved in stories that were passed from generation to generation and in the collective memory of the nation. Therefore there is less knowledge of the periods before the Israelite conquest than of the period from the conquest until Ezra (Esdras) and

Nehemiah - some 800 years. The fact that so many places in the land have preserved their biblical name or merely altered it slightly is invaluable in connecting the events and descriptions in the Bible to geographic and historic reality.

The Egyptian rule in Canaan, which began after the expulsion of the Hyksos tribes in the 16th century B.C., was expressed mainly in the occasional military campaign and in tax collection from the local rulers (ìkingsî in the Bible). Without a continuing central government, there were numerous conflicts between the local leaders, and occasionally they also joined forces with external powers. When several of them joined forces with the Hittites - the rising power in the north that threatened Egyptian hegemony - the Egyptian ruler, Thutmosis III, departed for Megiddo, where the rebel armies had gathered. In the great ensuing battle (1468 B.C.), which is documented in detail, the Egyptians routed their enemies with a mighty blow that deterred all attempts of rebellion for a long time.

During the Canaanite period, cities, which for security reasons were usually built on a natural hill, became the political units together with their environs. Upon their destruction, the remains of the fortifications and thick walls caused the hill to grow higher and gave the mounds their typical flat-headed conoid shape, which is so familiar to travelers in Israel. The construction of the walls, a weighty project, dictated the size of the cities, which were small and crowded and often had a population of only several thousands. Aside from the ruler and his men, the city was inhab-

ited by the wealthy classes, the merchants and artisans and their families. Farmers lived in the areas around the city and agriculture constituted the economic base of the town. The various populations in the city had different origins, and with time distinct classes formed. The term Canaanites was first used for merchants in the coastal towns, and with time became a general name for the land and its people. The

Excavating anthropoid-form burials south of Gaza (14th-13th cent. B.C.)

Canaanites did not accept the Egyptian religion and worshipped the gods of the land: El, his wife Ashra, and their son Baíal - the lord of rain and the source of life, and the son's wife, Anat - the goddess of fertility. The gods had human characteristics and did not constitute a source of inspiration in matters of justice and ethics.

The Egyptian records mention the Habiru (or

Megiddo, remains of the Canaanite temple with a round altar (2500-1850 B.C.)

Hapíiru) tribes - a general name for nomad tribes lacking any national identity that occasionally appeared from the desert. At the end of the 14th century B.C. the Hebrews emerged as an independent factor joining up with different kings and threatening Egyptian hegemony. There are those who view this as the first sign of the Hebrew people. It is possible that the mountain dwellers were called the Amorites even though they did not have a common ethnic origin, and they are the Amorite Kingdom mentioned in the Bible. On the eve of the Israelite conquest, Canaan was full of unrest and rebellion against Egyptian rule, in addition to the quarrels among the kings themselves.

Anthropoid sarcophagi excavated south of Gaza, dating from the late Canaanite period (14th-13th cent. B.C.)

The Israelite Conquest (end of the Bronze Age and beginning of the Iron Age)

The ancient stories of the Israelites were passed down from generation to generation until they were put in writing in the days of David and Solomon, some 250 years after the conquest of the land by Joshua. The changes and events that took place in the intervening time, as well as changes in the point of view of the Bible's writers, apparently caused discrepancies in the times recorded for the events and in the manner of their presentation. However, the Bible is still a highly reliable source for the names of places and the events described in it.

The emigration to Egypt, as well as the exodus from it, were not unusual events in the lives of nomadic tribes in that period, and apparently did not leave a lasting impression on Egypt. To this day no Egyptian evidence has been found of the event that plays such an important role in Jewish tradition. It should also be remembered that not all of the Hebrew tribes emigrated to Egypt, some of them remaining in Canaan. What is unique about their exodus from Egypt is the organized departure and the determination of their leadership, which acted so vigorously to consolidate the people and to impart religious and ethical values along with a complete system of laws and regulations.

The short route from Egypt to the Land of Israel passes along the shores of the Mediterranean Sea. It seems that the Children of Israel tried to pass that way but stopped when they encountered a series of Egyptian fortifications and took the long course that encircled the Sinai peninsula and ended in the southern part of trans-Jordan. Joshua made his conquests in several campaigns, at the end of which the mountain area of the Land of Canaan was in the hands of the Israelite tribes while the valleys and the Mediterranean coast remained under the control of the Canaanites and foreign tribes. The settlement in the mountainous area, which was uninhabited and far

The Ark of the Covenant on wheels, stone carving from the Capernaum synagogue

from the main roads, contributed to the inhabitants' feeling of security and to their consolidation into an economic political unit, which became a united sovereign entity 200 years later under the rule of David. During the interim, the connection between the tribes was not strong and varied between mobilizing to fight a common enemy and violent struggles between themselves. The constant unifying factor was the Ark of the Covenant and the structure which contained it, which was apparently situated at Shiloh at that time. All the tribes participated in its upkeep, and it served as a place of meeting and as the highest religious authority.

Several decades after the Israelite settlement, the Philistines arrived from the Greek islands and from Crete and settled in the southern part of the coastal plain. This invasion was part of the movement of peoples which took place in that period in the eastern Mediterranean basin, when tribes from eastern Asia invaded the Greek islands and their inhabitants abandoned them. Even though they never gained control of the Land of Israel, the Philistines were a constant bitter rival for the tribes of Israel, and their name was immortalized many centuries later when the Romans named the land Palestine in order to obliterate the name Judah. Even after the tribes united under King Saul (1020 B.C.) they were defeated by the Philistines in the battle at Mount Gilboa, where King Saul and his son Jonathan were killed.

King David managed to subdue them and to enlarge the young kingdom. The large empires in the region were undergoing a period of weakness, and David, who unified the tribes and made Jerusalem into the capital and religious center of the kingdom, turned to organizing his government and patterns of rule. It was a period of economic prosperity and cultural and spiritual creation that has been deeply stamped on the national consciousness of the people of Israel. Despite the opposition of his ministers, David chose his son Solomon to rule after him, and the forty years of Solomon's rule (970-930 B.C.) are testimony to the wisdom of his choice. Solomon succeeded in creating a system of alliances and commercial ties with the neighbouring countries, developed the government and tax collection systems, disbanded the mercenary army and established a mobile unit on chariots, built the Temple in addition to great construction and fortification works. The growing tax burden caused unrest among the people, and towards the end of his reign, Solomon saw the beginnings of the undermining of his kingdom.

After Solomon's death the kingdom split in two: the kingdom of Judea, which included Jerusalem and its environs and the tribes of Judah, Simeon, and Benjamin alone, under the rule of Rehoboam son of Solomon (930-914 B.C.) ; and the northern kingdom of Israel, which included the rest of the tribes, under the rule of Jeroboam, a bitter enemy of Solomon in his lifetime. During the following two hundred years, the area saw the ascent and decline of military and political powers, conquests, wars and varied alliances. The two kingdoms managed to survive, sometimes cooperating with each other and sometimes not, until in 732 B.C. Israel was conquered by Tiglath Pileser III, king of Assyria. Many of the residents were exiled to distant Assyrian provinces, and were replaced by inhabitants from other lands conquered by the Assyrians. Israel's attempts to renew its independence lasted another 12 years through joining rebels in Assyria and not cooperating with the conqueror, until

Sargon the Assyrian conquered Samaria, exiled many of the inhabitants and completely destroyed the Kingdom of Israel. Judah alone remained, and in face of Assyria's overwhelming superiority, was forced to pay it tribute.

Babylon, the new power to the east, vanquished Assyria and turned west to the eternal rival - Egypt. The Babylonian campaign passed through Judah, Egypt's ally, and in 587 B.C. Nebuchadnezzar conquered Jerusalem, destroyed the city and the Temple and led thousands of the land's inhabitants to captivity, leaving behind him a kind of Jewish autonomy, under the rule of members of the royal family. The ties between this community and the exiles in Babylon were very close.

Only 48 years passed until the next upheaval - the conquest of Babylon and its empire by the Persians. The tolerance which characterized Cyrus (559-530 B.C.), king of the Persians, who allowed various nations to continue observing their religious customs and allowed war refugees to return to their homelands, was applied to the Judahite exiles in Babylon as well. After his victory Cyrus issued a declaration that allowed the rebuilding of the Temple in Jerusalem, the return of the Jews in Babylon to Judah, and the sending of donations from Babylon to Jerusalem (538 B.C.). The rebuilding of the Temple was completed in six years (515 B.C.), but the small stream of returning exiles gained momentum with the arrival of Ezra the Scribe 60 years later, and became significant only when he was joined by Nehemiah, who was a minister in Cyrus' court and was given wide authority. Nehemiah became a governor on behalf of the king of the Judah area, and together with Ezra diligently maintained its Jewish character, a fact that fashioned the image of Judah for many generations to come.

Cast of seal inscribed "Shema, servant of Jeroboam," found in Megiddo (Jeroboam II, King of Israel; 8th-7th. cent. B.C.)

The Hellenistic Period

In the middle of the 4th century B.C., a new force appeared in the scene - Alexander The Great, who conquered the area in a storm and brought a new governmental and cultural world to the east. Because of the rapid conquest, the rulers of the new empire did not succeed in establishing orderly rule over wide areas, and after a period of chaos following Alexander's death, three kingdoms consolidated in the region. The Kingdom of Ptolemy, based in Egypt, the Kingdom of Seleucus, the largest of the kingdoms, which covered most of the areas of the Persian empire, and the Kingdom of Macedonia (under Antigonus), the mother-state of the conquerors. In order to establish their conquest and to strengthen their rule, the Hellenistic kingdoms required professional people in

9

all fields and brought them from Greece. This led to the spread of the Greek language, culture and life-style in the area.

During the 3rd century B.C. the Hellenistic states prospered: the security, the development of science and the Greek lifestyle - including the creation of cities with the encouragement of the authorities - brought economic prosperity. In the following century, ties with the mother-state grew weaker, the number of those coming from there diminished, the Greek minority was exposed to eastern traditions and cultures and its influenced waned. Judea, which was defined as a nation dwelling around its Temple, enjoyed autonomy under the rule of the High Priest and the Council of Elders who were authorized to manage it according to the laws of the Torah.

The continuous influence of Hellenistic rule was expressed mainly in the material culture: coins, architecture and art. The number of Jews in the country grew, some of them settled outside the autonomous area, and many were given Greek names. Connections with Diaspora Jews, mainly in Babylonia and Egypt, were very close, and great effort was made to preserve the unity of traditions and religious rituals. The Land of Israel was the boundary area between the Seleucid Kingdom to the north and the Ptolemies to the south, and changed hands several times as part of the power struggles between the two states. However, in times of peace it benefited from being the crossroads of commercial routes in the area.

At the beginning of the 2nd century B.C., the Seleucid state had financial difficulties because of its heavy debts to the newly expanding Roman state and many military expenses. Therefore Antiochus Epiphanes (175-164 B.C.), on his way back from a war campaign to Egypt, decided to seize the treasures of the Jewish Temple. The Jewish wave of rebellion, which came as a reaction to the pillage, led Antiochus to declare a religious war on the Jews, and as a first step he settled many foreigners in Jerusalem. When the Jewish mutiny continued, Antiochus increased his pressure and declared a complete ban on Jewish religious observance in all of Judea, and forced the Jews to participate in offering sacrifices to the gods of Greece. These steps were unprecedented in their severity and only few Jews obeyed them. Many left Jerusalem for the provincial towns, where governmental supervision was lax. One of these was Mattathias the Hasmonean, a priest who had returned to his town of Modiîn and who stabbed one of the Jews participating in offering sacrifices. Immediately afterwards Mattathias escaped to the mountains with his five sons and began organizing armed resistance to the government. At the outset it was a guerrilla war in which the Hasmoneans took advantage of their mobility, their knowledge of the terrain and the aid of the local inhabitants to defeat the army of Antiochus time after time. In 164 B.C., Judas, named Maccabeus, son of Mattathias, commander of the Hasmonean army, conquered Jerusalem and purified the Temple. However, the war was not over, and in several battles the Hasmonean army suffered heavy losses and was even forced to retreat from Jerusalem. A large military force under the command of Nicanor which was sent to remove the Hasmonean threat was defeated by Judas, and Jerusalem returned once again to the hands of the Jews. In order to strengthen his position, Judas made an alliance with Rome, but the Seleucids returned to the arena with strengthened forces under the command of Bacchides. In a battle at Baíal Hatzor where the quantitative advantage was on Bacchides's side, the Hasmonean army was defeated and destroyed almost entirely, and Judas Maccabeus fell in the battle.

Bacchides returned to his country and Jonathan, a younger brother of Judas, who had managed to escape with some of his men, returned to fight the reduced Seleucid army. Making clever use of the intrigues in the Seleucid court, Jonathan succeeded in obtaining from the Seleucid ruler, Alexander Balas (150-145 B.C.) recognition of his position as leader of the Jews and as High Priest, a position that the Hasmoneans were to hold for 115 years. In 129 B.C. the military campaign of the Seleucids against the Parthians failed, the Seleucid kingdom fell apart and the peoples of the area gained their independence. The main threat to the Hasmoneans were the Nabateans in the south, but the conquest of the southern part of Trans-Jordan by John Hyrcanus (135-104 B.C.) the Hasmonaean removed that threat as well, and the Hasmonean kingdom then entered a period of consolidation and growth. The Hasmonean state reached the height of its strength and size during the days of John Hyrcanus' son, Alexander Janneus, and at the time of his death in 76 B.C. it included the Land of Israel, the Golan heights and the western part of Trans-Jordan. Queen Salome Alexandra, the wife of Alexander Janneus who ruled after his death (76-67 B.C.), preserved his achievements, but the continuing disputes between her sons, Hyrcanus and Aristobolus, facilitated the conquest of the country by the Roman army under the command of Pompey in 63 B.C.

Caesarea, aerial view of the port today, built by King Herod in 23-13 B.C.

Roman Rule

The Romans, who recognized the special character of the Jewish kingdom, did not annex it to the Syrian province, but appointed Hyrcanus the Hasmonean as High Priest, and placed their collaborator Antipater the Idumean (Edomite) at his side. From the very beginning, Roman rule met with fierce opposition from the Jews, who saw the Roman Empire as the epitome

Rome, Arch of Titus: the triumph and the menorah, spoil from the Jerusalem Temple after destruction

of evil which must not be compromised with. Herod, the son of Antipater, who was first appointed governor of Galilee, was recognized by the Romans as the King of Judea and assisted them in finally overrunning Judea in 37 B.C. Even though his family had been converted to Judaism for several generations, in the eyes of the Jews Herod remained a foreigner, and his heavy-handed methods of ruling only increased the hostility towards him. During the 33 years of his rule (37-4 B.C.), Herod invested most of his resources in an unprecedented building momentum. He built new cities: Sebastia in Samaria and Caesarea along the coast, with a port that is considered one of the great building projects of ancient times. Herod built fortresses and palaces, roads and aqueducts, public buildings and hippodromes. The crown of his work was the expansion and renovation of the Temple, which won acclaim even from his Jewish enemies. After the death of Herod the country was divided among his three sons, but in face of the continuing resistance of the inhabitants, the Romans decided to appoint Roman governors to different counties.

The struggles and tensions, between the Jews and the Roman authorities, and no less between the Jews and non-Jews, reached a state where a clash between Jews and Hellenists in Caesarea in A.D. 66 ignited the Great Revolt of the Jews against the Romans. In reaction to a campaign of murder and robbery, during which the Roman soldiers plundered the Temple, the Jews took control of Jerusalem. Violent riots broke out in all the mixed cities in the country, and following the oppressive campaign of Gallus, the Roman governor, many joined the revolt. The Jews organized themselves for war. Many fighters were enlisted, fortresses were strengthened and the country was divided into three commands. In 67 A.D. the emperor Nero sent his highest ranking commander, Vespasian, at the head of an army of 60,000 soldiers to put down the revolt. Vespasian arrived from the north, and systematically conquered fortress after fortress, until finally in 68 A.D., all that remained in the hands of the Jews were Jerusalem and several fortresses in the Judean desert and in Trans-Jordan. The Jews did not succeed in reaching a unified control of their army, and the Jewish leadership was divided and full of intrigues. At this stage Vespasian had to return to Rome where he became emperor, but internal disputes among the Jewish leadership prevented them from exploiting the respite and improving their position. Vespasian's son, Titus, who was sent to complete the suppression of the Revolt, required only a few months to place Jerusalem under siege, break down its walls, conquer the Temple Mount and destroy the Temple (A.D. 70). One month later the upper city also fell and the Revolt was completely suppressed. Three fortresses, among them Massada near the Dead Sea, held out, and three more years were required to overcome their imposing fortifications and determined defenders.

Rabbi Yohanan ben Zakkai, who opposed the Revolt, was smuggled by his pupils out of Jerusalem before it fell, and settled in the coastal town of Jabneh together with other leaders who were brought there by the Romans. Even though many Jews were killed or taken captive during the Great Revolt, the economic damage was relatively small since the battles were waged around the fortified places and not on cultivated land. The mountainous and Galilee areas remained inhabited by Jews and the Romans preferred to preserve the Jews' organizational structure over social and religious chaos. Therefore, the Romans allowed the reestablishment of the Sanhedrin in Jabneh, headed by Yohanan ben Zakkai, and it became the source of new religious rulings which were suitable for a people without a Temple, of regulations regarding the cultivation of land, and mainly of hope and strength of faith for the defeated people. This period, called the Jabneh Generation, which lasted until A.D. 132, had great im-

Dead Sea Scrolls: the "Temple scroll" from Qumran

portance in the history of the Jewish people. During this period, modes of life and religious practice suitable for a people living under foreign rule were consolidated, and in effect prepared the Jews to preserve their religious and cultural uniqueness when they were dispersed around the world and were forced to live in small communities.

The longing for freedom and renewed Jewish independence did not disappear, nor did the spirit of rebellion and hatred of foreign rule. Evidence of this can be found in the revolts of the Jews in North Africa and Cyprus in A.D. 115-117 which also spread to the Land of Israel. The visit of Emperor Hadrian in A.D. 129 awakened great hopes for the renewal of Jewish Jerusalem among the Jews, who saw him as an enlightened and friendly emperor. However Hadrian decided to leave the 10th Legion in Jerusalem where it had been stationed since 70, turning it into a Roman city - common practice in the Roman Empire - and thereby started the process which brought on the next revolt, the Rebellion of Bar Kochba. The lessons of the Great Revolt were learnt by Rabbi Akiba, the spiritual leader of the rebellion, as well as by Bar Kochba its military leader. Preparations were made covertly: money was collected in the country and abroad, arms were manufactured and collected, strategic points were fortified, the army was trained far from Roman eyes, and many hiding places were dug, connected by tunnels. The Rebellion's beginning, A.D. 132, was set for the time when Hadrian was visiting a distant area of the Empire. It is suggested that in the first stage the rebels conquered Jerusalem, built a temporary Temple, renewed civil government and even minted coins. The slow-moving Roman army, which had difficulty withstanding Bar Kochba's swift elusive army, suffered heavy defeats and in one battle even lost an entire legion - a rare occurrence in the history of Rome. After they reorganized, the Romans began to systematically reconquer the area, by paving roads from one vantage point to the next, in order to achieve complete control over the war. The area controlled by the Jews grew smaller and smaller; in A.D. 134 Jerusalem was conquered and the final stronghold of the rebels, Bettar, fell in A.D. 135 after a long and difficult siege. In order to prevent additional attempts at rebellion, the Romans embarked on an especially cruel campaign of destruction: hundreds of settlements were destroyed and hundreds of thousands of Jews were massacred or exiled. In effect the Jewish settlement in Judea was almost annihilated. The Jewish settlement in Galilee, which suffered less from the results of the Rebellion, was subject to harsh edicts which in effect forbade the practice of Jewish religious and cultural life.

As time passed, and despite the strengthening of the Jewish settlement no signs of rebellion appeared, the Romans lightened their hand. In A.D. 212 the Jewish religion attained recognition when the Jews received Roman citizenship and authority over the cities and areas where they lived. The economy of the Jewish settlement was based mainly on a class of independent farmers and on the manufacture of olive oil, cloth and weapons. In the third century Rome underwent a continuous crisis, which caused increased taxation on the inhabitants of the empire and infighting and anarchy in the army. Because of their economic straits, many Jews emigrated to Babylon, but the Land of Israel still did not cease to be a center of Torah study, along with other centers in Babylon, and remained a focus for the redemption longings of the Jewish people.

Christianity

The split between Judaism and Christianity began immediately after the crucifixion of Jesus. The first Christian evangelists saw the Jews as natural candidates for receiving the faith, but they met with decisive resistance.

Several Jewish communities accepted Christianity as an additional faith and their members, who were

Bronze bust of the Emperor Hadrian found at Beit She'an

called minim were considered traitors by most of the Jews. This phenomenon did not continue very long, and the polarity between the two faiths became an established fact.

In the third century the civilized world was ripe for new tidings, after the values of the old world had lost their meaning, and at a certain stage both Judaism and Christianity were candidates to fulfill this need. Despite certain similarity in the ideas that the two monotheistic religions preached, Judaism - which obliges its believers to maintain a demanding framework of life with many commandments and a defined nationality - did not win many followers whereas Christianity spread rapidly. In 324 Constantine defeated his rival, Licinius, and became the first emperor of Rome who tolerated Christianity. Constantine viewed the converting of all the empire's inhabitants to Christianity as a mission of utmost importance and began to act in this spirit in the Land of Israel, at first in a moderate manner. His son, Constantine II (337-340), increased the pressure and added edicts and restrictions, and his successors continued in this spirit, until finally in 415 the institution of the Jewish Patriarchate, which was the highest authority for the Jews in the country and abroad, was canceled. The Jewish settlement was separated when the country was re-divided into Palestina Prima, which included Judea, Samaria, the Negev and, later, part of Trans-Jordan, and

The mosaic floor from the church of "the Loaves and Fishes" in Tabgha (Sea of Galilee), symbolizing the miracle of Jesus

Palestina Secunda, which included Galilee and the former Decapolis cities. Despite all the above, the Jewish settlement succeeded in preserving its spiritual independence and maintaining its ties with the Jews of the Diaspora.

The Persians, the ancient rival of the Byzantines - the Eastern Roman Empire, once again approached the country after their overwhelming victory over the Byzantine army. The hopes of the Jews for an improvement in their situation were reawakened . In 614, the Persians conquered the Land of Israel, and the Jews helped them as best as they could. Although the Persians gave Jerusalem to the Jews at the beginning of their short-lived rule (614-629), under the pressure of the Christian environment their policy soon changed and the Jews were once again expelled from the city. Heraclius the Byzantine emperor, who reconquered the country in 629, placed the Jews outside the law as retaliation for their support of the Persians, and the Christians slaughtered the Jews of the land mercilessly. Most of the Jews who managed to survive the massacre escaped abroad, and only a small, non-influential Jewish settlement remained.

The Arab Conquest

The four hundred years of war between Persia and the Byzantine Empire weakened the two powers, and Muslim Arab tribes, arriving from the deserts of Arabia, imbued with the new religious fervor of Islam, quickly gained control of large parts of their territories. During the years 634-640 the Muslims conquered the Land of Israel, Syria and Trans-Jordan. Even though the Jews, Christians and Samaritans, like all the non-Muslims, were treated as lower-class citizens, the authorities maintained a fair and equal attitude towards them as the People of the Book. During this period Tiberias was the spiritual center for the Jews of the country and the Diaspora, and Torah study took place there, as well as the laying down of religious laws, study of traditions, creation of literature and poetry, and, above all, the rules of Hebrew vocalization, which are valid to this day. As the years passed more and more Jews immigrated to the Land of Israel, and some of them joined the Jews of the land who had settled in Jerusalem and its close environs. When the tradition of pilgrimage to Jerusalem became widespread for Jews, Christians and Muslims alike, the city's importance grew, and at the beginning of the 11th century the Rabbinical academy, the highest authority on Jewish religious law in Palestine, moved to Jerusalem. The largest Jewish community was in Ramleh, the administrative capital of the Palestine District, and there were other communities in Hebron, Tyre, Acre, Caesarea, Jaffa and Ashkelon. For the Muslims and for the Christians, the city was a religious center, but with lesser political importance.

The Crusades

From its early beginnings Christianity had a strong affinity for the Land of Israel, and pilgrimages to the Holy Land were known already in the 4th century. In about 800 the Emperor Charlemagne built a hostel and a monastery in Jerusalem in order to serve the growing stream of pilgrims, and in the 11th century convoys of hundreds of people organized and made their way by land or sea. In the middle of the 11th century the Seljuks - Turkish tribes from mid-Asia who converted to Islam - invaded large areas of the Byzantine Empire, and almost reached Constantinople.

At that time, holy wars were being conducted in

Europe against the Muslims, in Spain and Southern Italy, and the request for help that the Byzantine emperor sent to Pope Urban II found a ready ear. In his appeal to Christians to come to the aid of their brothers in the east, the Pope included the vision of the redemption of Jerusalem and the Holy Sepulcher from the hands of the 'infidels'. The first to answer the call was a mixture of destitute farmers, fugitive law-breakers, knights with no inheritance and others with nothing to lose. They set out in 1096, and their path through the Rhine and Danube valleys was fraught with cruel acts of robbery and massacre of Jews. The reaction of the inhabitants further on along the way was more aggressive, and measly remainders of these gangs reached Constantinople.

The First Crusade included four camps of knights: from Provence, Southern Italy and Sicily, Northern France and Lorraine, and North-Western France. When they arrived in Constantinople, the knights quarreled with the emperor, who demanded that all the territories that they would conquer should be given to him, and they set out without his consent. The journey from Constantinople to Jerusalem lasted three years; the Crusaders' main enemy was the difficult road, since the Muslims could not gather enough forces to significantly challenge them. Of the hundreds of thousands who left Europe, only some 20,000, a small minority of them fighters, reached Jerusalem. The Crusaders laid a five-week siege to Jerusalem, but they themselves suffered from the heavy heat, the lack of water, food and arms and could not at first conquer the fortified city. Fortunately for them, a convoy of Genovese boats arrived at that time in Jaffa, bringing reinforcements who made their way to Jerusalem, and built siege machinery of wood from trees that they cut down in the area and from their dismantled boats. And thus, on 15 July, 1099, Jerusalem fell to the Crusaders, with the Jews fighting against them shoulder to shoulder with the other residents of Jerusalem.

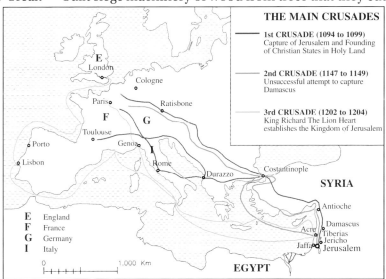

Map of the first three Crusades

After the conquest, the Muslims and Jews of Jerusalem were cruelly massacred, the Muslim world was in turmoil, and there was no real power that could oppose the Crusaders, who continued with their conquest of the Holy Land, from Tiberias in the north to Jericho in the east, and established a presence that was to last two hundred years.

Two basic conditions were necessary for the existence of the Crusader kingdom: control of the coastal cities in order to allow for a sea connection with the mother-countries, and the creation of territorial continuity which could be defended from the Muslim enemy. The fleets of the Italian maritime cities recognized the opportunity and swiftly came to their aid in both conquering the coastal cities and in creating regular supply and trade routes with Europe. In return they received extensive trade rights and quarters in the coastal cities that were conquered. The Crusaders achieved a state of co-existence with the rulers in Syria in the north, and to the east they took control of extensive territories in Trans-Jordan, as far as the desert in the east and Eilat in the south.

The country was divided into princedoms which drew their authority from the king of Jerusalem, like the feudal system in Europe. These included the signiors, estates that belonged to knights who took part in the Crusade, and whose lands they farmed or leased out. The central governing institution was the Assembly of Knights, which had the authority to decide in fundamental matters such as taxes, political agreements or war campaigns, and also constituted a tribune for settling legal matters between the big vassals. In return for land the vassals undertook to place at the king's disposal a set number of knights, fully provided with arms and horses, and this they did by allocating part of the land to additional knights. Other institutions were the Orders of the knights - associations of knights who organized for specific purposes connected with pilgrims: medical treatment, lodging and protection. These associations were connected to parallel organizations in their country of origin, which supported them with money and manpower, and with time the associations took on a national character. The consolidation of the kingdom drew immigrants from Europe: merchants, freed farmers and artisans. Most of the immigrants lived in the cities, while the village dwellers were largely Syrians - local people who had remained faithful to their Christian faith even during the Muslim conquest. Muslims and Jews who survived in the kingdom did not suffer from discrimination and had equal rights to those of the Syrians. When the maritime connection to Europe became regular, Jews began coming to the Land of Israel, some as pilgrims and some to settle.

Saladin, who at first was the army commander of the Seljuk kingdom in Syria and then the ruler of Egypt, set out to fight the Crusaders, but at a battle that took place at Gezer in 1174, suffered a severe defeat. He devoted the next ten years to gaining control of Syria in order to prevent a renewed alliance between that country and the Crusaders, and when he felt sure of his authority and the strength of his army, he went to

Belvoir, sculptured head of a Crusader soldier

war once again. The Crusaders were not prepared, and in the battle at the Horns of Hattin on July 4 1187, their main military force was defeated by Saladin. The downfall of the rest of the kingdom took several months, and in October of that year, Muslims prayed in the Omar mosque in Jerusalem once again. Saladin encouraged the Jews to return to Jerusalem, also as a demonstrative act against the Christians, and at the beginning of the 13th century Jewish settlement was renewed in the city.

The fall of Jerusalem sent shockwaves through Europe, and subsequently the largest Crusade (the Third Crusade) was organized. In 1191 the Crusaders came to Acre and laid siege to the Muslim city, while behind them they were surrounded by an additional ring of forces under the command of Saladin. The siege that lasted two long years drew the attention of the entire world, and finally the Crusaders conquered the city and the road south, along the coast, was open. After stalking the rear of the Crusader army along the way, Saladin faced Richard the Lion Heart for the decisive battle at Arsuf. Though the Christians won this battle, they did not have the strength to conquer Jerusalem, and the two exhausted combatants reached an agreement, which was signed at Ramle and announced the establishment of the second Kingdom of Jerusalem. It was a highly reduced kingdom, which included only the coastal area and lacked a real basis for its existence. In 1228 and in 1249 additional Crusade campaigns took place in an attempt to maintain and strengthen the Crusader kingdom, but they met with only partial success.

Crusader period metal vest from ancient Akko, 8 miles north of Haifa

The Mamluks

The Mamluks were slaves who were acquired by Saladin and his successors (named the Ayyubids after Saladin's forefather) when they were still boys in non-Muslim countries. After they accepted the Muslim faith, they received military training in order to serve in the armies of Muslim countries. They were organized in separate regiments, and since their position was dependent on their military skills, they achieved high command positions and were able to exploit their influence in politics. In 1249, when the Egyptian ruler died and no successor was appointed, and with the threat of a Crusader invasion, the members of the Mamluk regiment stationed on an island in the Nile rebelled and put forward their own candidates to rule.

In 1260, Baybars, a Mamluk commander, defeated the Mongol army

Kala'at Namrud, engraved script dedicated to the fortress governor, Elmalic El-Aziz, Saladin's nephew, dated A.D. 1229

which had conquered Iraq and Syria and had invaded the Land of Israel. Afterwards he turned to annihilating the Crusaders. One after the other, Baybars' army conquered the cities and fortresses of the Crusaders. This reconquest took a few decades to accomplish. Finally Acre was conquered in 1291 and its inhabitants cruelly massacred. The Christians evacuated the coastal cities and escaped to Cyprus. In order to prevent a renewed Christian invasion, Baybars destroyed the coastal towns and razed the ports. The coastal plain stood abandoned for many years and the center of settlement in the Land of Israel was concentrated in Galilee, Samaria and the Judean mountains.

The key positions in the civil government were given to military men in order to make it efficient and practical. Baybars developed a fast equine postal system in order to be in close contact with what was going on around the kingdom. For this purpose roads were paved, stations for changing horses were built, road inns were constructed. The Mamluks were very extreme in matters of religion and glorifyied Islam by building mosques, schools, hostels for pilgrims, monuments and magnificent family graves. Baybar's successors continued his building momentum, which included renovations in Jerusalem and the Temple Mount, and many of the structures then built may be seen to this day.

At the end of the 15th century the number of Jews immigrating to the Land of Israel increased, most of them Spanish refugees who were escaping from the harsh persecution that reached its climax with the expulsion of all Jews from Spain in 1492.

Muslim rule in the Land of Israel, which lasted some 900 years until the Ottoman conquest - with the exception of the Crusader period - brought it to a state of continuous decline. At the time of the first Muslim conquest in 638- about a millennium earlier - the country was inhabited in its entirety, and according to estimates and archeological findings, the population numbered several millions. The first census that the Ottomans held found that at that period only some 300,000 people dwelled in the country (of them some 10,000 Jews). The migration of large Arab tribes that passed through the country on their way west to North Africa and north to Syria caused long periods of disorder and lack of security. The central government, on the other hand, never ascribed great importance to the country itself, aside from its being a potential battle arena.

The Ottomans

From the second half of the 15th century onward the Ottomans (originating from central Turkey) grew stronger, compared with the general decline that began in the Mamluk-Egyptian kingdom.

In 1453 the Ottomans conquered Constantinople from the Byzantines, and following that, the Balkan countries to the west and Kurdistan to the east. The Mamluks, who felt the encroaching danger, were forced to recruit Bedouins to serve in their army, and these tribesmen brought in a rough, undisciplined element. The discovery of the maritime route from Europe to India caused great damage to Egypt, which had been a critical passage point in the trade between

east and west, a fact that greatly contributed to its economy.

The tension between the Ottomans and Egyptians increased, and the balance of power shifted towards the Ottomans, who adopted the use of firearms, while the Mamluks claimed that men of honor do not kill their enemies from afar. When the Ottoman sultan Selim I conquered several princedoms in Asia Minor, the Egyptian army advanced towards him in order to investigate his intentions. Confrontation was in-

The Dome of the Rock mosque, built over the site of the Herodian Temple; the "Wailing Wall" in the foreground

21

evitable, and in the great battle which took place at Marj Dabik in Syria in 1516 the Mamluks were defeated. The Ottomans continued southward in a campaign that ended a year later with the conquest of Cairo with no significant resistance. After the conquest, the Land of Israel became part of the Damascus Province and was divided into five districts. At their prime, until the end of the 16th century, the Ottomans succeeded in stabilizing the system of government, which contributed to economic development and the security of the inhabitants and thereby to an increase in their number. However, only several decades after the conquest, the increasing corruption among the government and military people caused negligence and sloppiness in administration, leading to a decline in security and to grave economic regression. Bedouin tribes that occasionally raided the country disrupted the trade and badly damaged the agricultural infrastructure, while the government was unable to prevent these phenomena. In several cases the Bedouins gained control of wide areas of Galilee and established an independent governmental entity for considerable periods of time.

With the Ottoman conquest of the Land of Israel, the Jews' hopes for an improvement in their situation grew in light of the positive attitude which the refugees from the Spanish expulsion (1492) had encountered when they arrived in Turkey. The first who emigrated from Turkey to the Holy Land were Spanish refugees, and they were joined by Jews from the Ottoman Empire, as well as from North Africa and Italy. They numbered only several thousands, but they constituted a significant contribution to the small Jewish community. The main beneficiaries from this immigration were Safed and several Jewish settlements in its environs. The security in the area was good, the commerce was lively, and a cloth manufacturing and dyeing industry developed there. The goal of the rabbis and learned men who concentrated in Safed was to create a Torah center which could also provide certification for the Rabbinate and thus ensure continuity and development in the study of Jewish tradition. The objection of the Jerusalem Jews prevented the Jews of Safed from obtaining certification rights, but the flourishing of rabbinic creativity in Safed did not cease, and in the middle of the 16th century Joseph Karo wrote the Shulchan Aruch, the book of laws and customs which was accepted as a binding document by Jews around the world. Safed's proximity to the grave of Rabbi Shimon bar Yochai, putative writer of the Zohar, the basic book of Jewish mysticism, attracted Kabbalists from all parts of the Diaspora, and their work became the foundation of a new stage in Jewish mysticism.

In 1831 the country was conquered by the Egyptian ruler Ibrahim Pasha, who made great efforts to establish fair and efficient administration. Despite this, his government was not well received by the Muslim population, mainly because of the obligatory conscription into the army which he enacted. In 1834 the Bedouin Rebellion broke out and was cruelly suppressed, and this added to the bitter feelings against the government. The revolt of the Druze in Syria which came afterwards, brought about the intervention of the Turkish army, which lost its battle with the Egyptians. The road north was open to Ibrahim Pasha, but now, for the first time in the modern era, came the intervention of the European powers, which were anxiously monitoring the declining Ottoman Empire. Army forces from England, Prussia, Austria and Russia took control of Beirut and Acre and forced the retreat of Ibrahim Pasha, who left ruin and destruction behind him. In 1840 the Turks returned and took control of the Land of Israel, meeting with no opposition.

The disintegration of the Ottoman Empire brought about greater involvement of the European countries in the area. Their consulates in Jerusalem were important political bodies, mainly a source of security to their citizens residing in the country. Most of the Jews in the Land of Israel lived on contributions that were collected in the Diaspora with the purpose of maintaining Jewish life and religious study. In the middle of the 19th century, several attempts were made by Jews to change this way of life and to settle in villages, and the English philanthropist Sir Moses Montefiore petitioned the sultan in support of these efforts, but did not succeed. Montefiore, who saw the difficult conditions under which the Jews lived within the walls of the Old City, built the first neighborhood for them outside the walls, and in 1856 the first inhabitants moved in. Within twenty years additional neighborhoods were built west of the Old City, and most of the Jewish residents of Jerusalem lived in them.

Zionism and its Realization

The first agricultural settlement in the modern Jewish settlement was the Mikve Yisrael agricultural school, which was founded in 1870 by the Alliance Israelite Universelle, a French Jewish society that acted to promote Jewish education. The goal of its founders was to train professionals in the different areas of agriculture, who would create a productive life for Jews in the Land of Israel. The harsh pogroms against the Jews of southern Russia in the 1880s provoked an awakening and strengthening of the Zionist idea, whose main aim was the renewal of independent Jewish life in the Land of Israel. A number of Jewish groups were formed and pioneers came from eastern Europe to build new villages. Zionist movements began to be organized in various countries, which brought about the creation of Political Zionism expressed in the First Zionist Congress in 1897, under the leadership of Theodor Herzl.

The new villages suffered from many difficulties as a result of the settlers' lack of experience, the lack of financial backing, the hostile environment and the absence of an economic infrastructure in the country. The French Jewish baron, Edmond de Rothschild, came to their help, and for many years supported the settlements with money, management and the purchase of lands for the construction of new villages.

At the beginning of the 20th century the immigration of Jews was modestly renewed. However, the difficulty of adapting to life in a remote and neglected corner of the crumbling Ottoman empire, deterred most of them from staying in the country. Towards the end of World War I the British army, coming from Egypt, conquered the Land of Israel from the Turks, and in 1917 the Balfour Declaration was published, proclaiming Britain's willingness to assist in the establishment of a National Home for the Jews in the Land of Israel. Britain received a mandate to rule over the Palestine from the League of Nations, but despite the fact that the gates were open and the atmosphere was favourable - the number of Jews who came was modest. As time passed, the British government's consistent activities to develop the country, as well as the organization of the Zionist Movement's settlement institutions, led to an increase in the immigration of Jews and in Jewish settlement. However, this also caused an exacerbation of the conflict of interest between the Arabs and Jews in the country. Following an uprising in 1936-39 by the country's Arabs (who increasingly referred to themselves as Palestinians) and responding to the pressure of the pro-Arab British Foreign Office, the British government laid down strict restrictions on Jewish immigration, the purchase of land by Jews and their building of new settlements. This trend reached its climax after World War II, when the British did not allow hundreds of thousands of Jewish Holocaust survivors to emigrate to the Land of Israel. The Jewish settlement in the country, with the aid of world Jewry, acted on three levels: opposition to the British rule of the country and continuation of the settlement; organization of illegal immigration by land, sea and air; and political and information activity around the world.

On November 29, 1947, the United Nations took a decision to establish two states in the Land of Israel - one Arab and one Jewish. On the following day bloody riots broke out between the sides. The conflict reached its climax with the invasion of the regular armies of the surrounding Arab countries on May 15, 1948, the day the last of the British left the country and the Jews proclaimed their declaration of independence. The difficult war lasted many months, and in the summer of 1949 armistice agreements were signed between the young country and its neighbors.

The bitter conflict is not over. After several wars there now seems to be a possibility of settling it by negotiations. This may bring peace to the area, whose extensive upheavals are only partially recorded on these pages.

THE CITY OF DAVID

Jerusalem is first mentioned in Egyptian documents from the twentieth and nineteenth centuries B.C. The city was built in this period on a low narrow hill south of the later Temple Mount, chosen because of its proximity to the abounding Spring of Gihon (Virgin's Spring). The first inhabitants of the city preferred proximity to the spring over the defensive advantages of a fortified city, particularly since the eastern, southern and western sides of the hill were sufficiently steep to defend the city. Eventually the rulers of Jerusalem in the eighteenth century B.C. were obliged to surround it with a wall, 2.5 meters thick, parts of which have been exposed and can still be seen today. Much later, in order to ensure a continuous supply of water during a siege, a vertical shaft was dug, connected to an older channel leading to the Virgin's Spring. The date of the shaft has not been conclusively determined; it is generally believed to have been dug toward the end of the rule of Solomon or one of his successors.

During the first years of his reign, David consolidated his rule in Hebron, which served as his administrative and military center. Only after seven years did he feel ready to achieve his aim of unifying the tribes of Israel into one kingdom. The first step was to create territorial continuity between the two tribes - Judah (his own tribe) and Benjamin (a neutral tribe with no links to any other tribe) - and David did this (around 1000 B.C.) when he conquered Jerusalem from the Jebusites.

In this period the royal palace stood in the northernmost corner of the city, close to the steep eastern slope. David resided in this palace (perhaps the "Citadel of Zion" in the Bible) and enlarged it. He created a large artificial mound, with layers of stairs, at the head of which stood the palace.

When King Solomon moved the religious and administrative center of the city to the Temple Mount, the artificial mound lost its importance and stood barren until the days of King Hezekiah (8th century B.C.), when living quarters were built on its slopes. This mound is the most important remnant of the City of David. In his effort to prepare for the advancing Assyrian army,

Hezekiah's tunnel,
built at the end of 8th cent. B.C.

The Siloam inscription on the wall of Hezekiah's tunnel.

Inscribed stone weight found at Jerusalem (7th cent. B.C.)

in addition to strengthening the city's fortifications, King Hezekiah turned to solving the problem of water supply during a siege. In order to prevent the enemy's access to the water of the Spring of Gihon, and to ensure a large quantity of water for the city's inhabitants, Hezekiah decided to cover the mouth of the spring and to bore a tunnel which would lead the water to a pool on the other side of the hill and inside the city. To save time, the excavation of the tunnel - 533 meters long - was started on both sides simultaneously, and was indeed completed with admirable speed and accuracy. The encounter between the two parties of quarrymen was commemorated with an inscription engraved on the wall of the tunnel: "Behold the excavation. Now this is the story of the excavation. While the excavators were lifting up the pick, each towards his neighbor, and while there were yet three cubits to excavate, then was heard the voice of one man calling to his neighbor, for there was an excess of the rock on the right hand and on the left. And after that, on the day of excavating, the excavators had struck pick upon pick, one against the other, and the waters flowed from the spring to the pool for a distance of 1,200 cubits, and 100 cubits was the height of the rock over the heads of the excavators."

The view of the city presented here is based on fragments of information collected during the many digs carried out on the hill. In this manner were discovered, for example, the northern of the two gate towers which leads to the spring, various water systems, and living quarters from the period of the First Temple. At the head of the Temple Mount, at the northern end of the hill, Solomon's palaces and the Temple can be seen. The transformation of Jerusalem into the capital of the Kingdom of Israel and the construction of the Temple imparted to the city its religious and historic significance for Judaism, Islam and Christianity.

General view of Jerusalem during King David's and King Solomon's time

JERUSALEM DURING THE SECOND TEMPLE PERIOD

Following the conquest of Jerusalem by the king of Babylon, Nebuchadnezzar, and the destruction of the First Temple (586 B.C.), many of the inhabitants of Judea, including the religious and political elite, were exiled to Babylon. Many Judean districts were abandoned and remained in ruins until the Return to Zion began some fifty years later.

All this changed when the Babylonian Empire was conquered by Cyrus king of Persia in 538 B.C. Only one year after his victory over Babylon, Cyrus issued a proclamation encouraging the Jews - among other nations - to return to their land, and they were encouraged to rebuild the temple. The proclamation served his political interests, since Cyrus was interested in an ally in this turbulent country; but for the Jews it was the beginning of a process of political and religious rehabilitation. The first returning exiles from Babylon, whose main purpose was to rebuild the Temple, met with many difficulties but succeeded in completing their task in 515 B.C., only seventy-one years after the destruction of the First Temple. Sixty years later, the religious leader Ezra the Scribe, followed by the political and military leader Nehemiah, came to Jerusalem and acted to consolidate and enlarge the Jewish entity in the land of Israel. This is customarily defined as the beginning of the Second Temple period, but another four hundred years of wars and government upheavals were to pass until the Temple and Jerusalem reached the height of their glory.

Selah' coins from the Bar-Kochba revolt (A.D.134) with the facade of the Second Temple in Jerusalem

Herod, king of Judea under Roman patronage, is the man most closely identified with the building and development thrust, which was perhaps the greatest that the country has known until our time. The 33 years of his reign, until his death in 4 B.C., were characterized by economic prosperity and iron-fisted political rule. Herod built new cities, fortresses for external defense and internal security, roads and water systems. However, with his activities in Jerusalem and the Temple Mount, Herod reached the crowning glory of his building enterprise. Sayings such as "Of the ten measures of beauty that descended on the world, Jerusalem took nine, and the rest of the entire world-one" or "He who has not seen Herod's Temple, has not seen a fine building in his life," show that the inhabitants of Jerusalem in that period also viewed it as the most beautiful city. Herod's massive building in Jerusalem damaged many of the previous

The Temple Mount built by Herod, King of Judea in the second half of the 1st cent. B.C. View from the eastern side

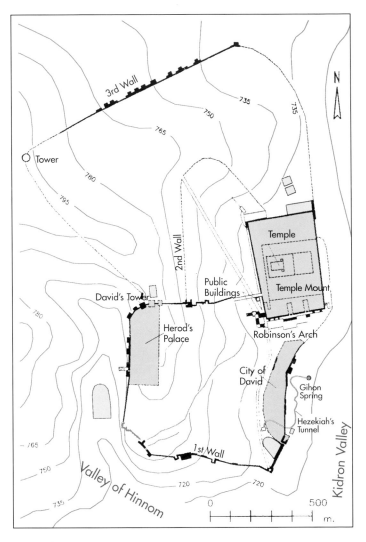

Map labels:
- 3rd Wall
- Tower
- 2nd Wall
- Temple
- Temple Mount
- Public Buildings
- David's Tower
- Herod's Palace
- Robinson's Arch
- City of David
- Gihon Spring
- Hezekiah's Tunnel
- Kidron Valley
- 1st Wall
- Valley of Hinnom
- N
- 0   500
- m.

structures; thus remnants from the period of his predecessors, the Hasmoneans, disappeared almost completely.

When Herod came to Jerusalem, it consisted only of the City of David, the Temple Mount and the Upper City, and was surrounded by the wall which Josephus Flavius called "the First Wall". This wall was originally built by the Hasmoneans, who in several places used remains of the fortification from the First Temple period. Herod improved this wall mainly by building towers, one of which - the Tower of David - stands to this day, and built an additional wall for the city - the Second Wall. The construction of the towers, as well as the fortification of the wall on the western side, were connected to Herod's palace, which was also built on this site. Herod apparently also built a central market and theater in this area, in addition to the public buildings which had already stood there.

The climax of Herod's endeavor was the rebuilding of the Temple Mount, with the Temple at its center. Here Herod demonstrated outstanding fortification ability: he not only enlarged the area of the Temple Mount, but also refashioned its surroundings by building gates and passages through its southern and western walls. He rebuilt the Temple itself almost entirely, and Josephus Flavius particularly mentions the southern Royal Portico (stoa), which was, perhaps, the most magnificent building that Herod constructed.

Map of Jerusalem at the end of the Second Temple period

THE ROBINSON ARCH

The Western Wall constitutes the retaining wall that surrounded the Temple Mount and supports the fills therein. Herod enlarged the area of the Western Wall by filling and leveling the ground, and apparently also by building vaults in certain places. Because of the topography, the wall which surrounded the renewed site was higher in the southern part where it reached a height of over thirty meters. The valley separating the western wall from the Upper City to the west was an obstacle in creating direct access to the Temple Mount. The problem was solved by building bridges and arches which connected the Upper City to the Temple Mount, over the valley, and led people to the Temple Mount level.

One of these passages is located close to the southern end of the Western Wall, and was discovered in 1838 by an American researcher named Edward Robinson, who identified the large arch stones protruding from the wall as an abutment of a bridge. Robinson assumed these belonged to one of a series of arches creating a bridge that connected the Upper City during the Second Temple period (the Jewish Quarter today) to the Temple Mount. Further research proved that Robinson's assumption about the bridge was wrong and that the arch was built during the construction of the Temple Mount by Herod as a single arch over the street. It was an enormous arch that leaned on one pier at a distance of some thirteen meters from the

The "Jewish wars" shekels (A.D. 66-70)

Western Wall. In the pier there were openings facing the street, and during the excavations stone and clay vessels were found there, as well as weight stones and coins from the Second Temple period. A wide staircase was built at the end of the arch, descending down to the street running alongside the Western Wall. This was one of the four gates to the Temple Mount and the Royal Portico for those coming from the Upper City and for pilgrims. The Royal Portico, which was accessible from the entry above the Robinson Arch, was an enormous, magnificent structure constructed along the entire length of the southern wall of the Mount. The Jewish historian, Josephus Flavius, who saw the arch with his own eyes, describes its details. He relates that the Temple Mount had four gates that opened to the western side, two of them onto the street. Excavations also revealed the paved street along the Western Wall under the arch, as well as many arch stones, stairs and banisters which apparently had remained there since the destruction of the Temple. The foundations of the arch were also found, and this made possible the reconstruction we see

The Western Wall (sometimes called the "Wailing Wall"), remains of the retaining wall of Herod's Temple, the most sacred site in the Jewish world

here. North of this arch another arch was found, (named after the archeologist, Charles Wilson), which was part of a bridge connecting the Upper City to the Temple Mount.

The need for many large gates to the Temple Mount resulted from the Temple's role as a center of the religious, social and political life in Judea. Three times a year, thousands of people came here to fulfill the pilgrimage commandment and to offer sacrifices. The administrative system that operated the Temple numbered hundreds of people in various jobs, aside from the priests who served in holy worship and played key roles in the social life of the people. Unlike in other religions, the Temple itself did not own land. The wages of the priests and the Levites, as well as the Temple expenses, were paid from tithes, donations and presents from the people. A tax of half a silver shekel per capita was always levied, as well, to finance the Temple expenses, and it is known that the Jews who lived outside the land of Israel also contributed their share.

The Temple's rituals were very strict and exact, as we learn from the abundance of instructions and regulations appearing in Jewish religious literature. It is possible that the colonnades surrounding the Temple's courts served the administrative system of the Temple, and during a certain period also housed the Sanhedrin.

Reconstruction of the western wall of the Herodian Temple-Mount with the big arch and the staircase which connected the temple to the city of Jerusalem. At right the Royal Portico and in the foreground a public or private building surrounding the sacred precinct

THE CARDO IN JERUSALEM

The Roman emperor Hadrian, who came to power some fifty years after the Great Revolt and the destruction of the Temple (A.D.66-70) chose to concentrate on consolidating the empire's economy and ensuring its borders, instead of his predecessors' policy of conquest. In A.D. 129 he visited the eastern part of the empire and traveled from Jericho to Jerusalem and Gaza. In anticipation of his arrival the road system was improved, and the Jews were full of hope that the emperor, who was considered moderate, would assist in renewing normal Jewish life in the country. Shortly afterwards, the emperor announced his decision to found on the ruins of Jerusalem a new city to be called Aelia Capitolina and to hand it over to the legion soldiers for settlement. The resulting disappointment and shock experienced by the Jews were among the causes of the bloody Bar-Kochba Revolt, which broke out three years later. The failure of the revolt in A.D. 135 brought with it the end of Jewish settlement in Jerusalem for several hundred years.

Jerusalem, terra-cotta storage jars of the Roman period

In Jerusalem, the Cardo was installed by Hadrian to serve as the main road in the heart of the city, crossing it from north to south. The meaning of the Latin name Cardo is axle - the Latin word itself originating from the Greek word cardos - "heart". According to the Roman plan the Cardo, a wide, straight road, was the central street in cities or military camps. The Cardo was first constructed in A.D. 135 by the Romans, builders of Aelia Capitolina. It begins at the Damascus Gate, which was magnificently built at that time, and from there leads southward to the center of the city, where it was to intersect the street leading from west to east.

In the sixth century A.D., the Byzantine emperor Justinian continued the construction of the road in the southerly direction. The extension had become necessary for two reasons. First was the increase in the number of the city's inhabitants and its expansion southward, which required improvements in the road system in the southern part of the town. The second reason was Justinian's construction of a large church

Reconstruction of Jerusalem's main street (cardo), built by the Roman emperor Hadrian in the 2nd cent. A.D.

in the southern area, the New Church of the Mother of God - the Nea in Greek. In order to hold religious processions between the Nea Church and the Church of the Holy Sepulcher, which also abuts the Cardo, it was necessary to continue the road southward. When the work was completed, the Cardo stretched from Damascus Gate in the north to Zion Gate, which was slightly east of the current Zion Gate.

The Cardo, with a total width of some 23 meters, included a central open road for pedestrians, cattle and wagons, and two avenues of columns, one on each side. The avenues were roofed with a covering supported on the street-side by the columns, and on the other side by buildings containing shops. The customary plan of a Cardo called for a row of shops on both sides; however, in Jerusalem, because of the topography in what is today the Jewish Quarter, there were at certain points stores on the eastern side alone. Drainage channels were built on both sides of the central road to draw off rain water and carry it to reservoirs that were built under the Nea Church and in the nearby neighborhoods..

Madaba: mosaic floor of a 6th cent. A.D. church showing the map of Jerusalem with the Cardo in the center

The Jerusalem Cardo also appears in the Madaba Map - a mosaic map depicting the Land of Israel and its environs from the sixth century A.D., discovered in the town of Madaba (the biblical Medvah) in Transjordan, which accurately depicts the main sites of the Holy Land and its vicinity.

CAESAREA

Caesarea was built on the site of the older townlet of Straton Tower, first mentioned in the letters of the Egyptian treasury official, Zeno, who disembarked at its harbor while en route from Egypt to Syria in the third century B.C. The remnants of the original settlement - which got its name from a king of Sidon called Straton - lie north of a wall built much later in the Crusader period. In 96 B.C. the city first came into Jewish hands when it was conquered by the Hasmoneans as part of to their goal to capture the country's coasts and develop its fishing and shipping activities. In 63 B.C., the Roman general, Pompey the Great, conquered Caesarea and declared it a free town under the authority of the Roman governor in Syria. The great acceleration in its development began in 22 B.C., when Herod gained control of Caesarea and began his colossal building project. Herod built a large planned city, based on Roman building practice, including a surrounding wall, a theater and hippodrome, temples and other imposing structures. The palace built there served the Roman governor of Judea. In order to carry fresh water into the town, two aqueducts were built from the foot of the Carmel mountain range. Many sections of these aqueducts are still visible today, and on one of the pillars an inscription carved by soldiers from the 10th Roman Legion can be seen. The climax of Herod's Caesarea (which he named for the emperor Augustus) was the port. Though all its secrets have not yet been revealed, it is now clear that this port was one of the most impressive building projects of the period.

Caesarea, aerial view of the Roman theater and of the wall with the towers

The continuous friction between the Jewish inhabitants of Caesarea and the non-Jews was not the immediate cause of the outbreak of the Great Jewish Revolt against Rome in A.D. 66, but when these conflicts grew bloody in Caesarea, they became the spark that ignited the flame. During the revolt, Caesarea was the base of the Roman general (later emperor), Vespasian: from here he set out to conquer Jerusalem.

Caesarea. Remains of the Crusader city's arched porticoes

The principal remnants of the town, where most of the modern restoration work has been done, are from the Crusader period. Caesarea was conquered during the first Crusader campaign (1101), and became part of the marine transport system along the coast. During the period of Crusader rule, the city's fortification system was built and rebuilt several times, most magnificently by the French King Louis IX (known as Saint Louis) in A.D. 1249. In 1265 Caesarea was conquered by the Mamluk sultan Baybars, who destroyed its walls to prevent any possibility of resettlement. The town and its environs remained in ruins.

In the past few years, efforts have been made to expose the Roman-Byzantine and Crusader cities and to restore many of the findings. In the picture one can see the eastern Crusader entrance to Caesarea (there were two additional entries - northern and southern). The eastern entrance passed over a drawbridge that would be raised to prevent entry when an enemy approached the city. Its supporting pillars have been preserved to this day. The wall stood behind the bridge, with firing ports threatening anyone who came near.

The entry itself was indirect - the gate was not exposed to direct attack and battering rams. In order to break down the gate the enemy would have to turn to the left. In this manner, exposed to fire from the wall, the thrust of the attack would be broken.

The gate itself was adorned with beautiful capitals, cornices and other architectonic features which also have been preserved. In the upper part there were installations for pouring flammable materials on the attackers. The gate was protected by a metal screen and shutter, whose tracks can still be seen on the doorposts.

The wall-system fortification of Caesarea, built on the shores of the Mediterranean Sea during the period of the Crusader rule (A.D. 1101-1265)

MASSADA

Massada - the last Jewish stronghold to hold out during the Great Revolt against the Romans in the first century - lies on top of a cliff in the Judean Desert some 500 meters above the Dead Sea. The hilltop is accessible only by steep paths that are difficult to climb and this made the fortress built at the top nearly unconquerable. According to the historian, Josephus Flavius, in the year 40 B.C., Herod and his family, together with several hundred of his men, fled to Massada in fear of the last Hasmonean king, Mattathias Antigonus.

Cosmetic utensils found in the Zealots' dwellings: kohl spoons, lid of a mirror, comb, and perfume bottles

Antigonus besieged them but Herod, forcing his way out of the siege, traveled to Rome in order to obtain Roman patronage, and several months later returned and raised the siege. After he defeated Antigonus and became ruler in 37 B.C., Herod built Massada as a fortress. The fortifications included a double wall 1,400 meters long surrounding the mountain, three towers, four gates, storerooms for food and arms, a system of channels and dams for the transfer of flood water and water holes for storage. The northern area of Massada is especially impressive. Here Herod built a private palace (as opposed to the large official palace that was built on the western part of the site) on three rock steps overhanging the chasm, which were leveled in preparation for the construction of the palace. A residential palace was built on the top step, and on the two bottom steps - luxury and entertainment buildings. South of these palaces Herod built an elaborate bath-house, in the finest Roman style. The main path leading to Massada passed under this palace, and after several turns reached the main gates.

After Herod's death in 4 B.C., a Roman garrison occupied Massada. When the Great Jewish Revolt against the Romans began (A.D. 66), Jewish zealots from Galilee arrived in Massada, took over the fortress and settled there with their families. After preparing them for habitation, they used the casemates in the wall as living quarters. They turned the palaces into headquarters and public buildings after making use of

Aerial view of the Palace-Villa of Massada, built in three tiers on the northern edge of the cliff. The upper tier contained living quarters; the other two tiers were for entertainment and leisure.

some of the building stones to improve the dwellings. Much can be learnt about their way of life from the many findings that were uncovered in the living quarters. During the revolt the place served as a refuge for additional fugitives.

After the conquest of Jerusalem by the Romans in A.D. 70, the Roman governor Flavius Silva set out to conquer Massada, one of the few places that was holding out. The Roman force included the 10th Legion, auxiliary troops and thousands of Jewish captives who served as a work force. Since there was no possibility of conquering Massada by direct assault, Silva laid a thorough, well-planned siege on the fortress. He surrounded the mountain with a siege wall in order to prevent passage, built eight camps for his army around Massada, and began to build a ramp on the western slope, on which a siege tower was constructed. The Roman siege on Massada ended in A.D. 73, when the siege tower that advanced up the ramp reached the wall. Battering rams began destroying the wall and the Romans set fire to the fortress. The commander of Massada, Elazar Ben Yair, then assembled all the fighters and their families, about 960 men, women and children, and in a dramatic speech called upon them to choose death as free men instead of Roman captivity. Josephus Flavius describes, based on the story of two women who hid and survived, how each man killed his own family, and then a lot was cast to determine who would be the last to execute the terrible deed.

The place was abandoned for hundreds of years, until hermits arrived in the Byzantine period and even built a small church and a monastery. However, over time the place was forgotten, and the renewed identification was made by two American researchers in 1838. Since 1953, when a survey was made of the site, extensive digs and excavations have been carried out at Massada, especially during the years 1963-1965. Today much can be learned about this special place, and many generations of Israelis have been raised on the stories of the heroic defenders of Massada.

Massada, a pair of leather sandals (1st cent. A.D.)
Arrowheads from the Roman siege of Massada

THE CHURCH AT MAMSHIT

The Nabateans (an Arab tribe) arrived in the Negev mountains area during the Persian rule, in the fifth century B.C. At the end of the first century, the Sicilian historian, Diodoros described them as sheep- and camel-raising nomads, who also lived from commerce in spices and perfumes, which they brought from the Arabian peninsula and from robbery. The key to their survival was their ability to control the scant water resources of the area - the location of the water holes that they dug remained secret. Toward the end of the first century their activity expanded and the Nabatean kingdom reached from the Gulf of Suez in the west to Edom in the east, and from the Hauran in the north to the Arabian desert in the south. The capital of the kingdom was Petra, later famous for the beauty of its tombs carved in rock. Important Nabatean cities were built close to their trade routes. Following repeated raids of Arab tribes, commerce grew weaker and the Nabatean economic and military strength diminished for some time. However, after some of the Arab tribe members were assimilated into the Nabatean people and order was restored to the area, a significant shift occurred in the nomadic way of life. From nomads and traders they became permanent settlers and turned to agriculture.

With the aid of an elaborate system of dams and channels they collected rainwater from vast areas and conducted it to agricultural plots, where they

Mamshit (Memphis), aerial view of the Nabatean city in eastern Negev

43

grew barley for animal feed, fruit trees and vines. The Nabateans also raised a new breed of horses. It was a cross-breed between a small, stocky Asian horse and a tall, swift Arabian breed; intricate stables have been uncovered. The Nabateans built dams in creeks, and the water collected was used by the inhabitants of the area, whose numbers increased in their cities. The new residential structures were spacious, two-storied buildings, adapted to the special climate of the area.

In A.D. 106 the Nabatean kingdom was annexed to the Roman empire without battle, and the areas it previously controlled were declared by the Romans to be "Provincia Arabia". The peace that followed this move led to economic prosperity, which reached its height during the Byzantine period. Christianity arrived in the Negev in the middle of the fourth century A.D., and was declared to be the state religion toward the end of the century. Aside from the main ritual connected with Jesus, a cult of saints and martyrs from among the early Christians developed. A special place was set aside in the churches for symbolic coffins in which relics symbolizing part of the sacred image were buried. The oil which was poured into these caskets and later collected in marked bottles became a highly sought item among pilgrims, many of whom passed here on their way to Mount Sinai.

Following the Muslim conquest in the seventh century, the settlements in the Negev grew sparse, and within 150 years the permanent dwellers had left the area and only Bedouin tribes remained.

Mamshit (Memphis) is one of the six cities in the Negev that the Nabateans built near the roads that led from their capital to the coast. It was apparently the last city they built, perhaps after the Romans took control of the kingdom. Mamshit had a northern, an eastern and a western church. The eastern church, the largest and oldest in the city - dating from the fourth century - is shown here. It is built at the highest point in town, which was also its historic core. The church belonged to a compound that also contained an entrance area with rooms attached, which perhaps served as a small monastery, and a bath-house for purification. A large cistern was dug under the entrance area.

The church itself is composed of a central aisle and two lateral aisles - northern and southern. Columns separate the aisles. The side aisles were paved with stone, and the central aisle with mosaic stones in simple geometric designs, which have barely been preserved. To the east of the central aisle was the apse, surrounded by benches on which the ceremonial attendants sat. Stairs led to the throne of the church dean. On both sides of the apse there were rooms. Remnants of the chancel screen that separated the worshippers from the apse can still be seen today.

Mamshit, inside view of the Byzantine Church, built in the 4th cent. A.D. on the ruins of the ancient Nabatean city of Memphis

THE CARDO IN BEIT SHE'AN

Beit She'an lies at a strategic point at the entrance to the Jezreel Valley - the natural passageway from Transjordan to the Mediterranean Sea - and close to the major highway known as the Sea Road, which ran from south to north. The city is first mentioned in Egyptian documents 3,900 years old, and research has found indications that it was fortified already 3,500 years ago. Until the thirteenth century B.C. the city was under Egyptian rule, expressed mainly in payment of taxes and the periodic presence of Egyptian delegations. This did not prevent a Philistine presence in the city or commercial ties with seamen from the eastern Mediterranean Basin. Although King David annexed it to his kingdom, Israelites did not settle here. The struggle for control over the area included the Battle of Mount Gilboa, which took place nearby, when the army of Israel was routed by the Philistines. After Beit She'an was conquered by Alexander the

Beit She'an, aerial view of the excavations

Great in the fourth century B.C., the city was called Scythopolis, in honor of the Scythian cavalrymen who served in the Ptolemaic army, and this name was preserved in the ensuing eras. Under Roman rule, Beit She'an became an independent city, part of an alliance of ten cities (the Decapolis). During the Great

View of the main street (cardo) of Beit She'an as it was in the 4th cent. A.D. The columned road linked the theater to the foot of the mound where the first city was raised

Revolt against Rome in A.D. 66, Jewish zealots attacked the city, but its Jewish inhabitants preferred to fight them alongside the gentiles. However, the non-Jewish citizens did not trust their neighbors, and cruelly slaughtered the Jews.

Beit She'an reached the height of its development during the Byzantine period (fourth-seventh centuries A.D.), and most of the remains we see today are from this time. The city extended over a large area on both sides of the Harod River, and when Christianity became the state religion (fourth century), Beit She'an turned into an administrative and religious center. In opposing the Muslim conquest in the seventh century, the city's residents destroyed the water systems in the area. This, however, did not prevent the conquest but brought about a severe economic regression, a reduction in the city's population, and a significant decline in its importance.

Mosaic of Tyche, city goddess of Beit She'an

A fierce earthquake in A.D. 749 destroyed the Byzantine city of Beit She'an. Many parts of the buildings remained in the place of their collapse, and this assisted in the process of restoration. In the Crusader period, in the Middle Ages and during the hundreds of years of Ottoman rule, Beit She'an was an isolated small town, and remained so until new immigrants settled there after the establishment of the State of Israel in 1948.

The Cardo (main street) seen in the picture led from the Roman theater to the central streets of Beit She'an. It was some 180 meters long, and was called the Palladius street, because of the inscription found there stating that the street's portico was built by the bishop Palladius, apparently in the fourth century A.D. The portico underwent a thorough renovation in the sixth century. The street is over 7 meters wide, with a deep drainage channel in its center. The vault above the channel is characterized by its unique paving pattern. The installations, such as shops, on each side of the street were raised very high - up to 280 cm - and were covered with mosaic. These installations were separated from the street by the portico, which supported the roof that stretched along the entire length of the street and protected the facades of the shops.

In the sixth century changes were made in the street; some of the shops were knocked down to make room for the construction of a semicircular patio, surrounded by rooms with mosaic floors. In one of the rooms, a mosaic was found

Architectural detail excavated in the Roman city

describing Tyche, the goddess of the city. In the Muslim period, water cisterns and various structures were installed above the street. Only ten shops have been excavated so far. There has been widespread pillage of stones in the area, and few remnants are to be found along the street.

Beit She'an, general view of the Roman theater

THE THEATER IN BEIT SHE'AN

Built in the third century A.D., the Beit She'an theater was relatively large, with an audience capacity of up to 8,000. Researchers believe that this Roman theater was built on the ruins of an older theater. The builders of the Roman theater took great pains in its adornment. The stones decorating the back wall of the stage were brought from a great distance - from Asia Minor and even Greece. The back wall was decorated in a fashion characteristic of Roman-style theaters: a two or three-storied structure, ornamented with pillars supporting magnificent cornices. Apparently, the theater could be covered with sheets of cloth canvas that created shade, to allow for shows in the daytime, which would otherwise be impossible in the climate of Beit She'an. Evidence of this can be found in the holes that were bored in the structure and provided support for the girders carrying the cloth. The theater was built in the accepted style of the West, as can be seen from the immense width of the front stage and the opulence of the main entry to the galleries. Along the central aisle, between the spectators' galleries, circular rooms were built, unlike what has been found in other theaters and whose purpose is unclear: they might have served to store visitors' clothing, or perhaps for the sale of food.

The spectators' entry and exit system is well preserved. The damage to some of the seats apparently resulted from the collapse of stones and pillars in the earthquake of A.D. 749 which destroyed the theater. Many stones from the theater building were appropriated by local inhabitants for building in other places, and the reconstruction was, therefore, carried out with re-chiseled stones.

The theater was first excavated in the 1960s. From 1986 onward, the excavation and renovation work has continued with the intention of making it a center for cultural performances.

Beit She'an, flower patterned architectural decoration

Reconstruction of the theater built during the reign of the Roman emperor Septimius Severus (A.D. 193-211): the large spectators' section, the flight of stairs and the entrance galleries as seen from the stage

BELVOIR (KOKHAV HAYARDEN)

Belvoir, whose conquerors likened it to an eagle's nest and which lies 500 meters above the Jordan valley, was settled during the period of the Second Temple and in the Byzantine period. During the era of the Second Temple, when there was a Jewish community in Babylon, great importance was placed on the exact dates of Jewish holidays and on the first day of the month. These were determined by the Sanhedrin in Jerusalem and the most efficient way of notifying distant communities was to light beacons, starting in

Belvoir, aerial view of the Crusader Castle, destroyed by Saladin in A.D. 1189

Jerusalem and from there in a series of fires on the summits of the highest mountains, all the way to the Jews of Babylon. The site of Belvoir was apparently one of the links in this chain.

At the beginning of the twelfth century, the Crusader princes of Galilee fortified the place, later they sold it, and in 1168 it came into the hands of Hospitaler knights. They constructed a well-planned fortress which became one of the most important strongholds in the chain of Crusader fortifications in the northern part of the country. Its builders named it Belvoir ("beautiful view").

A deep moat, which served as the initial defense system, was dug around the fortress. We see here a view of the castle from the west, with the drawbridge that was constructed over the moat. Passing over the bridge, one gained entry to the first fortification system, which was a square area surrounded by walls, adjacent to vaults that served as living and storage areas. The moat itself was prepared to become a bat-

Reconstruction of the west side outer fortification of the Crusader fortress of Belvoir, built around A.D. 1140

tle site during siege, and in time of need the fortress defenders could emerge from special openings at the bottom of the wall and fight the enemy who had penetrated the moat. Fortified towers were built at the corners of the outer wall and at the center of each wall. An inner fortress (the keep) was built in addition, with a tower in each of its four corners. The entrance to the inner fortification was indirect and protected. It was two stories high, and the upper story held the castle's church. From the remains found in the ruins, it can be seen that the church was built with great decoration and splendour.

Belvoir, gate of the inner wall of the Crusader Castle (12th cent. A.D.)

The purpose of a large tower, which was discovered east of the main structure, remains unknown to this day. Due to its poor state of preservation, it is difficult to know whether it was an external tower (barbican), part of the fortress itself, an observation tower overlooking the Jordan Valley, or perhaps part of the Muslim fortifications from the time when they besieged the fortress.

The army of Saladin, which invaded the area in the years 1180-1184, failed several times in its attempts to conquer the fortress. Following the Battle of Hattin (1187), in which the Crusader army was routed, the entire Crusader state fell to the Muslims, and only the fortresses at Safed, Tyre and Belvoir remained in Christian hands. Saladin then returned and laid siege to Belvoir. For eighteen months the defenders of the castle stood firm against the Muslim army. Saladin himself joined the besieging army several times, and was even forced to "apologize" for his failure and place the blame on the large quantity of snow and the faulty roads.

Eventually the Muslims used a unique method to conquer the Crusader fortifications whose walls they could not breach. A trained unit dug a tunnel under the eastern tower and supported its roof with wooden beams. When the tower foundations were supported by these wooden girders alone, they set fire to them (on 5 January, 1189), and the tower collapsed. Even then the defenders did not surrender, and entrenched themselves in the keep. Finally, the remaining fifty knights and four hundred warriors were forced to yield in return for Saladin's promise of safe conduct to Tyre.

In the following thirty years Muslim farmers resided in Belvoir, but the ruler of Damascus, receiving rumors of a new Crusade campaign, decreed that several Crusader fortresses be demolished, among them Belvoir.

In the early 18th century, Bedouins settled here, naming it Kaukab el-Hawa - "The Star of the Winds". It is possible that this preserved the name of the small Jewish town of Kochav, which was situated on the eastern slope during the Second Temple period. Several stones from this town with Aramaic inscriptions on them were used by the builders of the Crusader castle. North of the castle passes the pipe which carried oil from Iraq to the port of Haifa until 1948, and which Arab villagers set on fire many times during the uprising of 1936-1939.

HAMAT GADER

Hamat Gader is located in a small valley that lies between Gilead to the south and the Golan to the north. It is surrounded on three sides by the Yarmuk River, which runs through deep canyons on its way west to join the Jordan River. Hamat Gader is named after the ancient city Gader or Gadara, on the Gilead highway, just south of Hamat Gader. The Hellenistic city of Gadara, which was included in the Decapolis alliance of cities in Roman times, was built nearby. Today the Jordanian town of Um-Keis lies on this site.

Hamat is a Hebrew term for warm spa, and such pools provide the place with its unique character. In the small valley there are four mineral springs with varying degrees of heat, and one fresh water spring. The healing properties of the springs were known in ancient times, and the oldest piece of clay pottery that was found at Hamat Gader is from the end of the second millennium B.C. During the Hellenistic period the city grew and reached the height of its prosperity during the Roman period. At that time the baths, spas, theater and elegant public buildings were built. The bath-house buildings have been well preserved; they were in use for hundreds of years and are mentioned in various travel accounts. An English traveler who visited Hamat Gader at the beginning of the nineteenth century wrote of the baths and drew them in operation, but a researcher who was there at the end of the century found the place abandoned and in ruins, and uncovered only the foundations of the bath-house.

Jews apparently settled in Hamat Gader even before it was conquered by Alexander Janneus, the Hasmonean king (103-76 B.C.). When Herod ascended the throne he established colonies of Jews on the Golan, and this contributed to the Jewish settlement in Hamat Gader. In the second century A.D., scholars used to meet at Hamat Gader during the bathing season to hold their discussions there. Judah Hanasi (head of the country's Jewish community) also joined in this custom, as is mentioned in the Talmud.

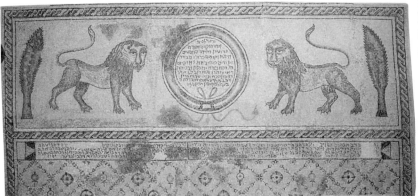

Part of a mosaic floor from Hamat Gader, now exhibited in the foyer of the Jerusalem Supreme Court building

The synagogue that was excavated at Hamat Gader is similar in its building style to other synagogues of the fifth and sixth centuries that were found in Galilee. It is generally thought to have been built in the fourth century A.D. A magnificent mosaic and several Aramaic inscriptions acknowledging the donors to the building - some of whom came from neighboring villages - were found on the floor of the synagogue. Today its floor is exhibited in the foyer of the Supreme Court building in Jerusalem.

After World War I Hamat Gader and the road leading to it were included in the area of the British Mandate, and during this period Jews and Arabs (mainly crowds of Bedouins) visited the baths. The Damascus-Haifa railroad track passed alongside the Yarmuk river, and one of the bridges of the track (which was blown up by Jewish underground fighters in 1946 during the struggle against British rule) can still be seen to the west of Hamat Gader.

In 1948, at the beginning of Israel's War of Independence, the Syrian army took control of Hamat Gader en route to its abortive attempt to conquer the Jordan valley. After the clashes Hamat Gader remained under Syrian control despite the truce agreement which included it in Israeli territory. As such the Syrians con-

The Hall of the Fountain, part of the Roman Baths complex built around the hot mineral springs of Hamat Gader

tinued to operate the baths and even improved them. During the Six-Day War Hamat Gader fell into Israeli hands. Today the site includes large areas of gardens and lawns and serves as a highly popular place of entertainment and therapy.

The baths, one of which appears in the reconstruction, were magnificently built and included a branched network of channels, pipes and tunnels that conducted the mineral and fresh water and drained the pools. They were apparently intended for notables and their families, and included large and small bathing halls, as

Hamat Gader, general view of the Roman Baths complex, using the sulphury hot-water springs

well as entertainment and rest rooms in the Roman style. The baths have undergone only partial restoration, but even so they are impressive in their scope and opulence. Some claim that these are the largest Roman baths to be discovered outside Italy.

THE CHURCH AT KURSI

During the paving of the road that ascends from the eastern coast of the Sea of Galilee to the Golan Heights, on the site where there had been an Arab village by the name of Kursi, a monastery was discovered, with a church at its center. Excavations carried out during the years 1970-1974 revealed that the place

Hamat Gader, detail of a water-channel for the bathing installations

was identified during the Byzantine period as Gedera, or the city of the Gadarenes, mentioned in the New Testament.

As related in the New Testament, Jesus arrived on this beach with the intention of escaping from the crowd which followed him everywhere and begged for help. According to Mark 5: 1-14: "And they came over unto the other side of the sea, into the country of the Gadarenes. And when he was come out of the ship, immediately there met him out of the tombs a man with an unclean spirit, who had his dwelling among the tombs; and no man could bind him, no, not with chains: Because that he had been often bound with fetters and chains, and the chains had been plucked asunder by him, and the fetters broken in pieces: neither could any man tame him. And always, night and day, he was in the mountains, and in the tombs, crying, and cutting himself with stones. But when he saw Jesus afar off, he ran and worshipped him, and cried with a loud voice, and said, What have I to do with thee, Jesus, thou Son of the most high God? I adjure thee by God, that thou torment me not. For he said unto him, Come out of the man, thou unclean spirit. And he asked him, What is thy name? And he answered, saying, My name is Legion: for we are many. And he besought him much that he would not send them away out of the country. Now there was there nigh unto the mountains a great herd of swine feeding. And all the devils besought him, saying, Send us into the swine, that we may enter them. And forthwith Jesus gave them leave. And the unclear spirits went out, and entered into the swine: and the herd ran violently down a steep place into the sea, (they were about two thousand) and were choked in the sea".

Kursi, a millstone from the monastery complex

According to tradition, this miracle occurred on the slope that lies south of the monastery. Pilgrims came here, and a small chapel was built.

Archaeological excavations have uncovered the walls which testify to the monastery's size (120x140 meters). Of the monastery itself, only the gate and several rooms, mainly near the northern wall, have been excavated. The monastery church was excavated in its entirety, and in its time was one of the largest churches in the country.

Built at the end of the fifth or the beginning of the sixth century A.D., the church was badly damaged during the Persian invasion (A.D. 614). Later it was repaired and continued to serve as a church until the eighth century; it is mentioned in travelers' stories. Later, an Arab settlement was established at Kursi, but it was soon abandoned.

The entrance to the church passes through an area surrounded by columns. Under this area, as was customary, a water cistern was dug to collect rainwater from the yard. Inside the church, the prayer hall was separated on both sides from the lateral aisles by a row of columns. In the aisles, there are mosaic floors with geometric designs; human and animal figures were apparently deliberately destroyed. On both sides of the lateral aisles there were chapels, also decorated with mosaics. The southwestern chapel served as a burial chamber. According to an inscription found in the southern room near the apse, this served as a baptism chamber at the end of the sixth century.

Kursi: reconstruction of the main hall of the Monastery-Church with the eastern side apse

THE SYNAGOGUE IN CAPERNAUM (KEFAR NAHUM)

Capernaum was a fairly large settlement on the northwestern edge of the Sea of Galilee from the time of the Second Temple onward. According to the New Testament, Jesus wandered between the fishermen and farmers in the area, preaching his gospel, working miracles and winning great admiration from the inhabitants. "And Jesus went about all the cities and villages, teaching in their synagogues, and preaching the gospel of the kingdom, and healing every sickness and every disease among the people" (St. Matthew 8: 35). Until the fourth century A.D., Jews and some Minim - Jews who followed Jesus - lived there, and gradually Christians settled there as well.

General view of the synagogue built in the middle of the ancient village

Over the centuries the place attracted many researchers, who were interested in the remains of its magnificent synagogue. During the years 1921-1926 the synagogue was excavated and partially restored. It is built in the pattern common in Galilee at that time (see below): lateral aisles along three sides, and three entrances on the open side facing Jerusalem. The synagogue hall was paved with large stone slabs. According to the numerous findings at the site, the building apparently had a second story, which may have served as the women's section. Even though the area is

Capernaum. View of the synagogue's prayer hall and of the second story women's section

The Sea of Galilee boat, dating from the 1st cent. A.D., excavated from the mud bottom

rich in basalt stone, the synagogue was built of limestone brought from the mountains of Lower Galilee, some six miles away. This is an indication of the generous investment in the building. The architectural sculpturing - the lintels, inscriptions, cornices, etc. - are also very rich. Many of these were damaged during later periods of iconoclasm - the destruction of images.

It is still unclear when the synagogue was built; the building style would lead to the assumption that it was constructed in the second or third century A.D. at the latest. However, numerous objects, such as coins, found by the Franciscans who conducted the excavations raise the possibility that it was built at a later date, perhaps even the fifth century A.D.

Many artifacts from the synagogue are to be found among the ruins, and Jewish subjects can be found among the numerous decorations and symbols carved on them. A seven-branched lamp along with a ram's horn and an incense burner - which served in Temple worship and became Jewish symbols - are carved on one of the pillars. A Temple-like object placed on a wagon is carved on one of the stone beams, possibly depicting the portable ark used during prayers in this synagogue (no installation was found in the synagogue to indicate that it was permanently located there). Dedication inscriptions to Jewish donors were found on two of the columns.

West of Kefar Nahum lies the valley of Tabgha, with numerous springs - some function as healing spas and some provide good irrigation water. Here Jesus performed two of his most famous miracles: feeding thousands of people with five loaves of bread and two fish (St. Matthew 14: 13-21), and his revelation to his fishermen disciples after his death (St. John 21: 1-17). For this reason, several small churches, which in time became magnificent basilicas, were built here in the fourth century A.D. Two of

Capernaum, remains of Peter's house

these, the Church of the Bread and the Fish and the Church of St. Peter's Seniority, which is near the shore of the lake, attract many visitors.

On a mountain slope to the north, where traditionally Jesus gave his Sermon on the Mount, lies the Church of the Blessed.

This church is built in the shape of an octagon, to commemorate the first eight verses of the sermon, opening with the word "Blessed". It was here that Jesus chose his apostles and appointed them to promulgate his gospel (St. Luke 6: 13).

KALA'AT NAMRUD (KALA'AT SUBEIBE)

The fortress known as Kala'at Namrud controls the road from Damascus to Tyre which lies south of Mount Hermon - the most convenient passage from Damascus to the sea. It also provides a magnificent vantage point over the Hula valley and southern Lebanon. The strategic location of the fortress placed it for many years at the heart of the political and military activity in the area.

Following their defeat in 1106, the Crusaders, in an attempt to move north with the aim of conquering Damascus, abandoned the city of Banias, which lay at the foot of Kala'at Namrud, to the Muslims. The people of the Muslim Ismaeliya sect, who received control of the area, felt threatened by Damascus, and in 1129 reached an agreement with the Crusader king, according to which Banias and the fortress would be handed over in return for protection for the people of the sect. That year, Baldwin II (De Burg), king of Jerusalem, arrived in the area, fortified the city of Banias and the fortress as well, and turned them into a front position on his road to the conquest of Damascus. Only three years later, the rulers of Damascus took advantage of the absence of the fortress's warriors, who had left to put down an internal conflict among the Crusader forces, and after a short battle captured the city and the fortress. De Burg's wife was among the captives. In 1137 the fortress was attacked and conquered by a Muslim rival of Damascus, who had arrived from the East. An agreement between the rulers of Damascus and the Crusaders promised the fortress to the Crusaders if they would come to the aid of Damascus in evicting the invaders. And indeed, in the famous Battle of Banias in 1140, which lasted an entire month, the allies prevailed and De Burg returned to the fortress with his knights. After repeated attempts, the city of Banias and the fortress were conquered by the Muslims in 1164.

The fall of the fortress was a severe blow to the Crusader kingdom. In 1217 an attempt to recapture it failed, and the last unsuccessful effort was made during the crusade of Louis IX in 1253. In 1260 it was conquered by the Mongols, but after several months.

In the early 16th century, when the area fell under Ottoman rule, it lost its importance, the fortress was abandoned and served as a shelter for shepherds and their flocks in the winter.

The remains visible today are of the fortress rebuilt by the Mamluks on the foundations of a previous, older structure. This reconstruction began in 1226 and continued for many years. The structure of the fortress is compatible with the topographic structure of the mountain range, and the building style which the Crusaders used is apparent in many of its parts. Because of the easier access from the south, the southern wall was fortified with seven protruding towers, in order to afford a wide field of vision and fire. The fifth tower is well preserved, with firing slits and an impressive entrance. The strong tower (the keep) - an inner, independent fortification - is at the eastern end, in the higher section of the fortress, and the gate leading to it is especially protected. Turning east at the entrance leads to the roof of a water pool, in the corner of the tower. Stables and carefully chiseled firing slits can be seen there.

Just north of the junction in the road leading to the fortress lies the tomb of a Druze sheikh, in the center of an oak grove 100-300 years old. As in other places in the country, the trees have been preserved because of their proximity to a holy grave, and therefore did not become goat fodder or coal. According to Druze tradition, the Sheikh Hazuri, a great peace lover, is buried here. He was in the habit of distributing a special kind of salt to travelers: to peace lovers it was tasty, while it would cause warmongers to lose their way and never reach their destination.

General view of Nimrod's Castle (Kala'at Namrud) with the castle in the background and the southern wall tower system in the foreground

TIBERIAS

Tiberias, on the western shore of the Sea of Galilee, was founded sometime about 18 A.D. on the site of the biblical Rakkath by Herod Antipas, the son of Herod. It was named after the emperor Tiberias, who was the patron of Herod Antipas (ruled A.D.14-37). The city was planned and built in the Greek urban style: magnificent public buildings, administrative institutions, amusement facilities and even an aqueduct for drinking water, 15 kilometers long, from the springs of the Yavne'el river. Tiberias held the customary powers of the "polis" (the ancient city-state) a controlled area, legislative authority and coinage rights. Since the city was built on a site that contained many tombs, and also because of their hatred for the Romans and their proteges, Jews were in no hurry to settle in Tiberias. In order to accelerate the process Antipas awarded the settlers many benefits, and also applied pressures. However, it was only when Antipas transferred his government center to Tiberias that it began to develop, and prosperous residents settled there.

When the Great Revolt against the Romans broke out in A.D. 66, Josephus Flavius, then the commander of Galilee, fortified Tiberias and prepared it for war. But when the Roman general, Vespasian, approached the city at the head of his army, the inhabitants decided to surrender without a fight. As a result, Tiberias was the only city in Galilee that was not destroyed in the war. After the destruction of Jerusalem and the Temple in 70

Kala'at Namrud, interior of a tower in the eastern wall

A.D., Tiberias' importance grew, and at the end of the second century it became the spiritual center of the Jews, both from the Land of Israel and from abroad. In Tiberias, the Palestine Talmud was completed at the beginning of the fifth century and it was in Tiberias that scholars determined the final text, pronunciation and vocalization of the Hebrew text of the Bible.

Christianity became the state religion during the days of the emperor Constantine in the fourth century

The 18th Century southern wall of Tiberias, built on the foundation of the Crusader fortification system.
In the background, the Sea of Galilee and the Crusader Castle on the hill

and in the fifth century a Christian community with a bishop was founded. Tiberias. In 614 the Persians invaded the country and the Jews of Tiberias, who had been persecuted under Byzantine rule, helped the Persians conquer their city.

However, Persian rule lasted only fifteen years, and when the Byzantines reconquered Tiberias, they revenged themselves on the Jews very cruelly.

The Arabs, who conquered the city in 636, turned it into an industrial and commercial center and the most important city in the northern part of the country. It continued to be a center of Jewish scholarship although in the tenth century the Jewish population declined and when the Crusaders conquered the city at the beginning of the twelfth century, only several dozen Jewish families could be found there.

Mosaic floor of the synagogue in Tiberias

Under Crusader rule Tiberias was the capital of the principality of Galilee. After the Crusaders were defeated by Saladin in 1187 in a crucial battle at the nearby Horns of Hattin, the Muslim army turned to Tiberias, conquered it after a siege that lasted about half a year, and laid the city in ruins. Tiberias changed hands several more times until it was conquered by the Mamlukes in 1247, destroyed and abandoned.

In the sixteenth century, after the Ottomans conquered the land, Jews began to settle once again in Tiberias. In 1562 Don Joseph Nasi, a Jew who had attained a high position in the Ottoman sultan's court, was awarded the city of Tiberias in order to settle Jews there and develop its economy. He restored the city walls and tried to consolidate the silk and wool industries. His attempt to do so failed and several years later Tiberias was once again abandoned. In the eighteenth century, the leader of the local Druze tribe, Dhaher al-Amr, took control of Galilee and began to restore Tiberias once again. He built a wall - the remnants of which can be seen today - apparently on the foundations of the Crusader wall. He made Tiberias his capital and invited Jews to settle there. Jews of Spanish and Portuguese origin came from Turkey and were joined by Hasidic Jews from Poland, and Tiberias became regarded as one of the four holy cities of the Land of Israel (together with Jerusalem, Hebron and Safed). Jewish settlement grew stronger until the year 1837, when an earthquake caused great damage and loss of life, and many fled the city.

The seven-branched menorah carved in limestone from the synagogue

Fresco depicting an angel found in the Byzantine church on Mt. Berenike, above the city

The city, which had throughout its history been situated along the seashore, began from the early 20th century to expand up the adjacent slopes where the greater part of the population now lives.

MEGIDDO

The Hill of Megiddo is situated near the exit from the Eiron valley, the most important mountain pass connecting the coastal region to the inland valleys. The city of Megiddo was founded at the end of the fourth millennium B.C., during which period the important towns in the country were established. The foundations of the wall that surrounded the city in that era (stratum XVIII), which were revealed in excavations, were eight meters wide and four meters high. Above it rose the wall, four meters wide and at varying heights. Temples from this period testify to the consolidation of city life. At the beginning of the second millennium B.C., Megiddo became one of the centers of Egyptian rule in the Land of Israel. During the rule of King Thutmose III (1504-1450 B.C.), Megiddo joined the alliance of kings of Syria, Anatolia and Mesopotamia that challenged Egypt's sovereignty in the area. Thutmose's vanguard army successfully surprised the rebels, and Egypt's victory in the heavy battle was complete. It is possible that the echoes of this conflict penetrated the Christian tradition, finding expression in John's vision where Megiddo beco-

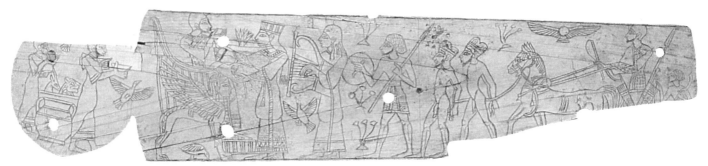

Ivory handle from Megiddo depicting a ruler, probably the king of the city, sitting on his throne and receiving a victory procession after a battle

mes Armaggedon: "For they are the spirits of devils, working miracles, which go forth unto the kings of the earth and of the whole world, to gather them to the battle of that great day of God Almighty... And he gathered them together into a place called in the Hebrew tongue Armageddon [in Hebrew Har Megiddo, 'the mountain of Megiddo']... And there was a great earthquake, such as was not since men were upon the earth, so mighty an earthquake, and so great; And the great city was divided into three parts, and cities of the nations fell" (Revelation 16: 14-19).

Following the systematic excavations carried out at Megiddo from 1925 to 1939, the hill became a key site in the understanding of Israelite culture during the Canaanite and Israelite periods. Researchers had the opportunity to understand the processes by which the Kingdom of Israel was founded, as well as the upheavals that took place with the conquest of the city by David, and especially with the building campaigns of Solomon. Megiddo is mentioned in the Bible as one of the cities that Solomon built (in addition to Jerusalem, Gezer and Hazor). Two fortresses from the period of Solomon were uncovered, in the northern and sourthern parts of the site, as well as the impregnable city wall with its gate, one of the largest and most imposing gates found in the country to date.

The Bible describes Solomon's extensive commerce with the neighboring countries, and especially his great wealth of horses, chariots and horsemen. This description, along with the fact that Megiddo was the seat of one of Solomon's governors, led researchers to assume that the remains of two magnificent stable systems that were uncovered are from the period of Solomon. Archaeological research carried out at the

Megiddo: proposed reconstruction of the so-called "King Solomon's stables"

Megiddo, the city gates built by King Solomon

site in the 1960s revealed a different picture. The prevalent opinion today is that the stables are from the period of King Ahab, who is also mentioned as the possessor of many horses and chariots. So as not to damage the unique structures, the excavators refrained from removing them, and the remains of Solomon's stables might lie underneath.

It seems, however, that one can learn about the structure of Solomon's stables from the arrangement of Ahab's stables. Aside from the monumental fortifications, the temples and palaces, the Hill of Megiddo is also characterized by its water works. Two access approaches were built to the spring that lies at the bottom of the hill, on its western side. The first approach, which served in times of peace, was a system of stairs that was built outside the wall, and parts of which may still be seen today. In order to reach the water in days of siege and war, a shaft twenty-five meters deep and twenty-five meters wide was dug, with stairs along its sides enabling water bearers to descend to the bottom. At the bottom of the shaft, a tunnel seventy meters long and three meters high was dug, carrying the spring water to the bottom of the shaft. From there the water was carried up in pails by the porters.

This was a complex and highly impressive engineering feat, meticulously planned, whose builders must have faced many difficulties during its construction.

After the Assyrian conquest, Megiddo continued to serve as the provincial capital, but following the Persian victory its importance diminished.

With the conquest of Alexander the Great, the town lost all historic importance.

Megiddo, public grain storage silo built by King Jeroboam

ISBN 88-8162-083-9

Archaeological Texts by Dr. D. Bahat
Paintings by S. Rotem
Design by U. Ulivieri
Photographs by Z. Radovan, Y. Tsafrit, D. Avni, S. Rotem
Produced by Vision S.r.l.   Via Livorno, 20 – 00162 Roma
                                            Tel/Fax (39) 06.44292688 – E-mail: vision.srl@stm.it

PAST & PRESENT®

Printed in Italy by: Tipolitografica CS - Padova